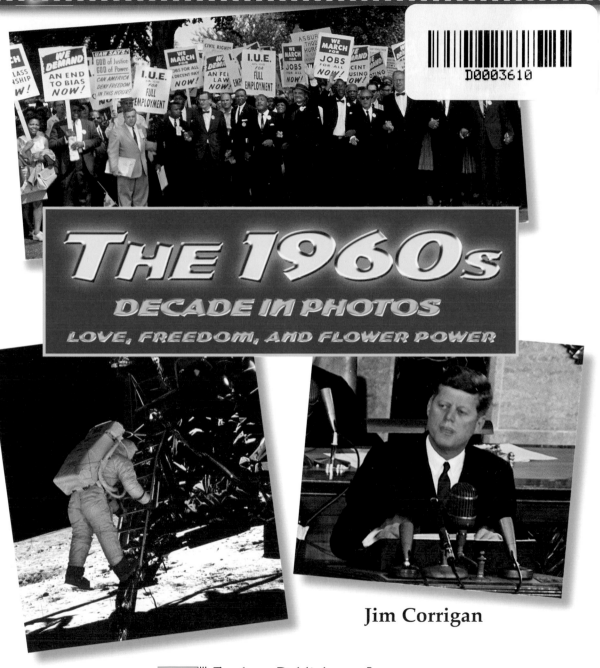

The 1960s
Decade in Photos
Love, Freedom, and Flower Power

Jim Corrigan

Enslow Publishers, Inc.
40 Industrial Road
Box 398
Berkeley Heights, NJ 07922
USA

http://www.enslow.com

Library of Congress Cataloging-in-Publication Data

Corrigan, Jim.
  The 1960s decade in photos : love, freedom, and flower power / by Jim Corrigan.
      p. cm. — (Amazing decades in photos)
  Includes bibliographical references and index.
  Summary: "Middle school readers will find out about the important world, national, and cultural developments of the decade 1960-1969"—Provided by publisher.
  ISBN-13: 978-0-7660-3135-7
  ISBN-10: 0-7660-3135-7
  1. United States—History—1961-1969—Pictorial works—Juvenile literature. 2. History, Modern—20th century—Pictorial works—Juvenile literature. 3. Nineteen sixties—Pictorial works—Juvenile literature. I. Title. II. Title: Nineteen sixties decade in photos.
  E841.C59 2009
  973.923—dc22

                                                                                                2008042996

Printed in the United States of America.

102010 Lake Book Manufacturing, Inc., Melrose Park, IL

10 9 8 7 6 5 4 3 2

To Our Readers: We have done our best to make sure all Internet Addresses in this book were active and appropriate when we went to press. However, the author and the publisher have no control over and assume no liability for the material available on those Internet sites or on other Web sites they may link to. Any comments or suggestions can be sent by email to comments@enslow.com or to the address on the back cover.

Every effort has been made to locate all copyright holders of material used in this book. If any errors or omissions have occurred, corrections will be made in future editions of this book.

♻ Enslow Publishers, Inc., is committed to printing our books on recycled paper. The paper in every book contains 10% to 30% post-consumer waste (PCW). The cover board on the outside of each book contains 100% PCW. Our goal is to do our part to help young people and the environment too!

Produced by OTTN Publishing, Stockton, N.J.

TABLE OF CONTENTS

Antiwar protesters in Berkeley, California, 1965.

WELCOME TO THE 1960s

The 1960s were a time of great tensions in the world. The United States and the Soviet Union were locked in a bitter rivalry. It was called the Cold War. The two countries did not fight each other directly. But they came dangerously close in 1962. If they had gone to war then, it might have spelled the end of the world. Both countries had thousands of nuclear weapons, and just one of these bombs could destroy an entire city.

During the Cold War, the B-52 was created to bomb targets in the Soviet Union. The American military tried to keep one-third of its B-52s in the air at all times. This way, the planes could still deliver their bombs even if their base were destroyed by a Soviet nuclear attack. B-52s were also sent on more than eight hundred missions to bomb targets in Vietnam.

Chicago police officers attempt to disperse demonstrators outside the Hilton Hotel, where the 1968 Democratic National Convention was being held.

Although they never went to war with each other, the Soviet Union and the United States supported opposing sides in many conflicts around the globe. One of these conflicts was in Vietnam. During the 1960s, American soldiers were drawn into bloody combat there. The Vietnam War turned out to be a long and painful struggle. The United States became deeply divided over the war. Some people questioned why American troops were fighting and dying in Southeast Asia. They called for the soldiers to come home. Others insisted that the United States should fight in Vietnam until the war was won. All the while, television showed gory scenes of the fighting.

But during the 1960s, Americans also saw disturbing violence in their own country. A president was shot and killed. As TV cameras rolled, his accused killer was himself murdered. Five years later, a presidential candidate was assassinated. So, too, was the country's most famous civil rights leader.

The civil rights movement reached its peak in the 1960s. Civil rights are basic freedoms. The Constitution requires that all U.S. citizens be treated equally. However, in the southern states especially, African Americans did not enjoy the same rights as white citizens. Segregation laws kept the races separate in the South. African Americans were forced to go to separate schools. They were not free to eat at the same restaurants as whites. They were not allowed to use "whites only" restrooms or drinking fountains. Other laws were designed to prevent blacks from voting. By 1960, African Americans no longer tolerated these laws. Their demands for equal treatment had grown into a national movement.

Young people were important to the civil rights movement. They also led a movement against the Vietnam War. They marched and protested. Sometimes, their demonstrations turned violent. On TV, Americans saw many scenes of young people clashing with police.

These clashes were just one sign of a deep split in American society during the 1960s. It was called the "generation gap." Many young people rejected the beliefs and values of their parents. They defied authority. They distrusted the government. Some of these young people were known as hippies. They had long hair, wore colorful and unusual clothing, and often took drugs. They spoke of peace, love, and "flower power" (nonviolence). Hippies made up a small minority of young people, and a small minority of people who protested during the 1960s. Still, the image of a hippie flashing a peace sign has become one of the most enduring symbols of that turbulent decade.

Civil rights leaders Martin Luther King, Jr., (1929–1968) and Malcolm X (1925–1965) speak together, 1964. Tragically, both men were assassinated during the 1960s.

U.S. Spy Plane Shot Down

America and the Soviet Union were Cold War enemies. Each side spied on the other. America secretly began using spy planes, the most advanced of which were called U-2s. The U-2s flew missions high over the Soviet Union to take pictures of military bases, missile launching pads, and other sites. On May 1, 1960, the Soviets shot down an American U-2 spy plane. It caused a major incident.

Francis Gary Powers (1929–1977) poses with a U-2 plane. He is wearing a pressurized flight suit because the U-2 could fly more than 70,000 feet above enemy territory.

The U.S. Central Intelligence Agency (CIA) ran the secret U-2 program during the 1950s and 1960s. The aircraft were used to spy on the Soviet Union.

At first, President Dwight D. Eisenhower insisted that the United States was not using spy planes. He said that a weather plane may have accidentally strayed over the Soviet Union and been shot down. However, the Soviets had proof. They found wreckage of the downed aircraft, including its camera. They also captured the American pilot. His name was Francis Gary Powers. The Soviet Union put Powers on trial for spying. He was found guilty. He was sentenced to ten years in prison.

Relations between America and the Soviet Union sank to a new low. Even so, Powers eventually returned home to the United States. In 1962, the Soviets traded him for one of their captured spies. After the U-2 incident, America began using spy satellites instead of planes. The satellites could take pictures from the safety of space.

Soviet president Nikita Khruschev examines equipment found in the U-2 wreckage at an exhibition in Moscow, 1960.

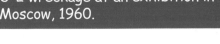

JFK Is Elected President

A NEW LEADER FOR THE 60's

KENNEDY FOR PRESIDENT

Poster for the Democratic Party's candidate in the 1960 presidential election, John F. Kennedy.

In 1960, Americans chose a new president. They elected John F. Kennedy. He was just forty-three years old. Never before had someone so young been elected president. Kennedy's energy and style uplifted the nation.

John F. Kennedy came from a wealthy Massachusetts family. In college, he was a fine athlete. Later, Kennedy served in the U.S. Navy during World War II. He was the captain of a small boat in the Pacific. His boat sank after being rammed by a Japanese destroyer. Kennedy received a medal for saving his crew.

In 1960, for the first time in history, television played an important part in the presidential election. Four debates between the two candidates were televised. Kennedy's performance helped him to pull ahead of Richard Nixon in public opinion polls.

"Ask not what your country can do for you," John F. Kennedy said in his inaugural address, "ask what you can do for your country." Sitting behind the president are Vice President Lyndon B. Johnson, and former Vice President Nixon.

After the war, JFK went into politics. He served in the U.S. Congress. He also wrote a history book. People respected his intelligence. Still, when Kennedy ran for president in 1960, many people doubted he could win. He was too young, they said. They also thought that his religion would hurt his chances. JFK was Catholic, and no Catholic had ever been elected president.

Kennedy surprised his doubters. He gave excellent speeches. He showed that he understood the challenges America faced. Young people especially admired him. The election was very close. But JFK defeated his opponent, Vice President Richard M. Nixon. Nixon would also become president later in the decade.

First Human in Space

Space exploration first began in the 1950s. America and the Soviet Union tried to outdo each other. This competition was called the space race. The Soviet Union took an early lead. It became the first nation to launch a man-made object into orbit. Then, in 1961, the Soviets achieved an even greater feat. They sent a human being into space.

An experienced Soviet pilot, Yuri Gagarin (1934–1968), became the first man to orbit the earth. His flight into space lasted about an hour and forty-eight minutes.

Russian astronauts are known as cosmonauts. Yuri Gagarin was a twenty-seven-year-old cosmonaut. He was chosen to become the first person in space. On April 12, 1961, Gagarin climbed aboard his spacecraft, *Vostok 1*. He blasted off and roared into orbit. Gagarin circled the planet once and then reentered Earth's atmosphere. He ejected from his craft and safely parachuted to the ground.

Yuri Gagarin instantly became a world hero. However, he would not enjoy his fame for long. He died in 1968 in a training-flight crash.

The April 12, 1961, issue of the *Huntsville Times* reports Gagarin's flight into space. At the time, America's rocket and missile program was located in Huntsville, Alabama.

Meanwhile, America scrambled to catch up with the Soviet Union. President Kennedy set the finish line for the space race. And he challenged America to get there first. "I believe that this nation should commit itself to achieving the goal, before this decade is out, of landing a man on the Moon and returning him safely to the Earth," Kennedy said in May of 1961.

Gagarin's flight gave the Soviet Union a lead of nearly a year in the Space Race. On February 20, 1962, John Glenn became the first American astronaut to orbit the planet. Glenn circled the Earth three times in a capsule called *Friendship 7*.

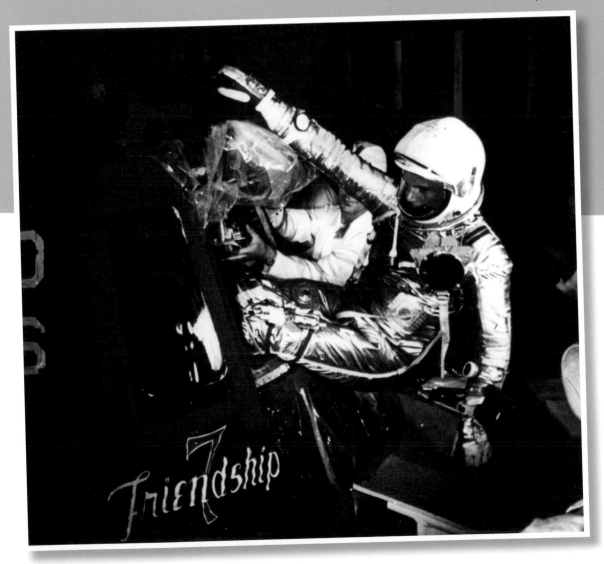

BAY OF PIGS INVASION

Cuba is an island nation. It is located just south of Florida. During the late 1950s, Cuba had a revolution. A new government came to power in 1959. It was led by Fidel Castro.

Soon Castro's government took property owned by American companies. It took land owned by rich Cubans and gave the land to poor people. Castro also turned to the Soviet Union, America's Cold War enemy, for aid. American leaders grew alarmed.

Many Cubans who disliked Castro's government moved to the United States. People who must leave their homeland are called exiles. Many of the Cuban exiles wished to overthrow Castro so they could go home. The U.S. government also wanted Castro out of the way. The Central Intelligence Agency (CIA) secretly began working with a group of Cuban exiles. The CIA gave them weapons. It also trained them for an invasion of Cuba.

The communist government of Cuban leader Fidel Castro had close ties to the Soviet Union. This worried U.S. leaders, who did not want the Soviets to gain influence in Latin America.

Cuban soldiers guard members of the invasion force who were captured in April 1961. Castro eventually agreed to let the prisoners go back to the United States. In exchange, Cuba received millions of dollars worth of food and medical supplies.

On April 17, 1961, the Cuban exiles launched their invasion. They landed at a place called the Bay of Pigs. But the invasion was a disaster. Castro's forces were ready. More than a hundred of the exiles died in the fighting. Almost all of the rest—about 1,200 men—were taken prisoner. The Bay of Pigs disaster embarrassed the United States and President Kennedy.

On December 29, 1962, President Kennedy met with Cuban exiles who had survived the Bay of Pigs invasion. The flag they are holding bears the nickname for the Cuban invasion force, Brigade 2506.

American soldiers search for a defensive position shortly after landing on a beach in Vietnam, June 1965.

U.S. Troops Go to Vietnam

The Cold War reached its peak in the 1960s. America and the Soviet Union were enemies. They competed fiercely for allies around the world. The two superpowers meddled in the politics of other countries. One of those countries was Vietnam.

Vietnam is located in Southeast Asia. For a long time, it was a French colony. After World War II, Vietnamese rebels fought for independence. They defeated the French in 1954. Afterward, the country was divided. In North Vietnam, a government headed by the rebel leader Ho Chi Minh was set up. Ho was supported by the Soviet Union. He wanted all of Vietnam to be a communist nation, like the Soviet Union and China.

Ngo Dinh Diem (1901–1963), the first president of South Vietnam, was not a good ruler. He ordered the police to arrest, torture, and kill his political enemies. He also appointed family members and friends to high-ranking government positions. Despite this, the United States supported Diem's government because he opposed communism.

American officials did not want this to happen. They helped Ngo Dinh Diem gain power in South Vietnam. Diem hated communism. Unfortunately, he was also a harsh and corrupt ruler.

By 1960, communist rebels supported by North Vietnam were fighting to overthrow Diem. American military advisers were sent to South Vietnam. The mission of these soldiers was to show Diem's army how to fight the communist rebels. It was a difficult job. Diem's brutality made him unpopular. More and more South Vietnamese people supported the communist rebels, whom the Americans called the Vietcong.

South Vietnamese troops direct civilians past the bodies of three dead Vietcong guerrilla fighters. The Vietcong were South Vietnamese rebels who wanted to overthrow Diem's government. They received help from North Vietnam's communist government.

In 1960, there were only nine hundred U.S. soldiers in South Vietnam. Within three years, the number had grown to more than fifteen thousand. They began doing more than just giving advice. They started battling the communists too. America was slowly being drawn into Vietnam's civil war. Before long, U.S. soldiers had taken a leading role in the fighting. The war continued to grow. North Vietnam sent troops and supplies into South Vietnam. America did the same. By 1969, over half a million Americans would be fighting in Vietnam.

U.S. troops found the war frustrating. Enemy soldiers used guerrilla tactics. They launched surprise attacks. Then they vanished before the Americans could fight back. Vietnam has thick jungles and grasslands. These were perfect places for enemy soldiers to hide. U.S. tanks and jeeps were of little use in the jungles. Instead, American soldiers moved around with helicopters and on foot.

The Vietnam War was very unpopular in the United States. Many people believed that U.S. troops did not belong there. They staged protests. College students were especially opposed to the war. They sometimes clashed violently with police. The Vietnam War made headlines throughout the 1960s.

During the early 1960s, American soldiers in Vietnam played a supporting role. They helped train the army of South Vietnam to fight the Vietcong. By 1965, however, U.S. troops were going into combat against the rebels and their North Vietnamese allies.

The "Rat Pack" Entertains America

A group of talented performers dazzled the nation in the early 1960s. These singers, actors, and comedians were close friends. They performed onstage together. They also made movies together. People called them the "Rat Pack." Their playful antics amused audiences.

Publicity photo for *Oceans Eleven*, the hit 1960 film starring the Rat Pack. Pictured are (left to right) Frank Sinatra, Dean Martin, Sammy Davis, Jr., Peter Lawford, and Joey Bishop.

Actor Humphrey Bogart was the original leader of a group of friends, including Sinatra, who became known as the Hollywood Rat Pack. Legend has it that his wife, Lauren Bacall, gave the group its nickname. After Bogart's death in 1957, Sinatra took over leadership of the group.

Frank Sinatra was the leader of the Rat Pack. Sinatra was born in New Jersey in 1915. His parents hoped he would become an engineer. However, young Frank knew he wanted to be a performer. As a teen, he sang in local talent shows. In the 1940s, he became a famous singer. Later, he also became an award-winning actor. Sinatra went by the nickname Ol' Blue Eyes.

Dean Martin and Sammy Davis, Jr., were also well-known members of the Rat Pack. Martin was an Ohio native. He held odd jobs before starting his singing career in 1939. He worked with comedian Jerry Lewis for many years before joining the Rat Pack. Sammy Davis, Jr., had been performing onstage since age three. As an African-American, he often endured racial slurs. He ignored the insults. Davis went on to become one of America's most beloved entertainers. Comedian Joey Bishop and actor Peter Lawford rounded out the Rat Pack.

President Kennedy discusses the Cuban Missile Crisis with some of his top advisors outside the White House, October 1962. Pictured are (left to right) Special Assistant McGeorge Bundy, the president, Assistant Secretary of Defense Paul Nitze, Chairman of the Joint Chiefs of Staff General Maxwell Taylor, and Secretary of Defense Robert McNamara.

THE CUBAN MISSILE CRISIS

Cuba once had friendly relations with the United States. But after the Cuban Revolution brought Fidel Castro to power in 1959, the country forged close ties with the Soviet Union. In late 1961, Castro announced that Cuba was a communist state. The following year, he agreed to let the Soviet

A U-2 spy plane took this photo of a medium-range ballistic missile launch site near San Cristobal, Cuba. This was one of nine launch sites planned to be built on the island.

1 NOVEMBER 1962

MRBM LAUNCH SITE 2
SAN CRISTOBAL

MISSILE-READY TENT

FUEL TRAILERS

FORMER LAUNCH POSITIONS

FORMER LOCATION OF MISSILE-READY TENTS

Union place nuclear missiles in Cuba. This sparked the Cuban Missile Crisis. For two weeks, the world drew ever closer to nuclear war.

A U.S. spy plane discovered the Soviet missiles being moved in Cuba on October 14, 1962. President John F. Kennedy was alarmed. Since Cuba is so close to America, the missiles posed a grave threat. They could carry nuclear bombs deep inside the United States without any warning. Kennedy knew he could not allow the missiles to stay in Cuba.

President Kennedy went on television. He let the world know about the missiles. He demanded that the Soviets remove them from Cuba. Kennedy also announced a "quarantine" of Cuba. U.S. Navy ships would form a blockade around the island, stopping and searching Soviet ships for missile parts. A blockade is a barrier created by ships at sea. Kennedy said that the blockade would stop more Soviet ships from taking missiles to Cuba.

Nobody knew how the Soviet Union would react to the blockade. Several tense days passed. Leaders from both sides realized the danger they faced. They could not let the crisis explode into a nuclear war. Quietly, Soviet and American diplomats began to talk. They worked to find a peaceful solution. Finally, on October 28, 1962,

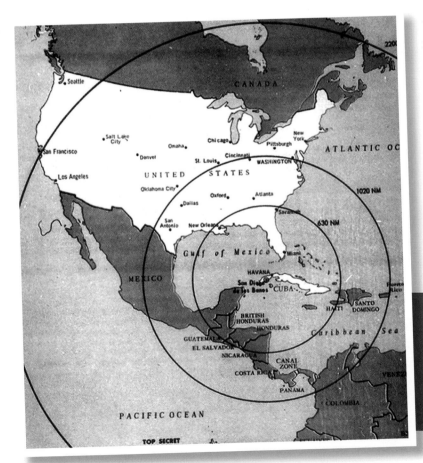

This CIA map, which was classified Top Secret in 1962, shows how missiles fired from Cuba could strike nearly any city in the continental United States.

Adlai Stevenson, the U.S. ambassador to the United Nations, shows maps and photographs of the Cuban missile sites to the UN Security Council, October 25, 1962.

Soviet leader Nikita Khrushchev gave a radio speech. He said that he would remove the Soviet missiles. In return, Khrushchev wanted a U.S. promise not to invade Cuba. President Kennedy agreed to this, and he also secretly agreed to remove American missiles that were in Turkey. Tensions began to recede. The crisis was over.

The Cuban Missile Crisis was a turning point in the Cold War. It taught both sides that they needed to use caution. In the years that followed, America and the Soviet Union carefully avoided further showdowns. They also held talks about limiting nuclear weapons. The Cold War would continue for three more decades. Yet the world never again came so close to nuclear destruction.

JFK Is Assassinated

President and Mrs. Kennedy arrive in Dallas, Texas, on November 22, 1963.

America's young president faced many challenges. John F. Kennedy guided the nation through the Cuban Missile Crisis. He inspired America to do better in the space race. People took comfort in his leadership. So they were especially shocked by the events of November 22, 1963. On that day, a sniper's bullets took the president's life.

President Kennedy and his wife, Jackie, were in Dallas, Texas. They were riding through the city streets. It was a sunny day and the car's top was down. The president and first lady waved as crowds of people cheered. Suddenly, three shots rang out. President Kennedy slumped forward. Two of the bullets had struck him in the

The Kennedys were accompanied by Texas governor John Connally and his wife, Idanell, as their limousine drove through Dallas. This photo was taken moments before the fatal shots were fired.

With a grieving Jacqueline Kennedy at his side, Lyndon Baines Johnson takes the presidential oath of office. This photo was taken on Air Force One about two hours after President Kennedy was killed.

head and neck. The car sped off to the hospital. Doctors were unable to save the president. His wounds were too severe.

News of the assassination quickly spread across the country. A stunned nation mourned. People struggled to understand why someone would kill the president. Meanwhile, Lyndon B. Johnson took the oath of office. He had been Kennedy's vice president. He became the nation's new leader.

Three-year-old John F. Kennedy Jr. salutes during his father's funeral in Washington, D.C., November 25, 1963. Americans were shocked and devastated by the death of their young president, who had brought a sense of hope and optimism to the White House.

PRESIDENT'S ASSASSIN IS MURDERED

The shots that killed President Kennedy came from a Dallas warehouse. An hour later, police arrested a worker from the warehouse. His name was Lee Harvey Oswald. The police said that he was the president's assassin. However, Oswald would never stand trial. Just two days later, he was murdered.

Oswald's reasons for shooting the president were never made clear. Lee Harvey Oswald was twenty-four years old. He had served in the U.S. military.

The Texas School Book Depository building is on the left in this modern view of Dallas's Dealey Plaza. The Warren Commission, an official investigation into the assassination, found that Lee Harvey Oswald had fired the fatal shots from the sixth floor of the building. However, some people do not believe that Oswald acted alone to kill the president.

Afterward, he went to the Soviet Union. Oswald wished to become a Soviet citizen. But Soviet officials denied his request. He returned to the United States in 1962. Eventually, Oswald got a job at the Texas School Book Depository in Dallas. Police said he was in that warehouse with a rifle when President Kennedy's car drove past. They said he shot the president.

On November 24, 1963, police were moving Oswald to a different jail. A large crowd was watching. There were news reporters and television cameras. Suddenly, a man with a gun stepped forward. He shot Lee Harvey Oswald in the stomach. Oswald died of the wound about an hour and a half later. Oswald's murderer was Jack Ruby. He said he was upset over President Kennedy's death. Ruby went to prison, where he died in 1967.

Dallas nightclub owner Jack Ruby (right) shoots Lee Harvey Oswald, November 24, 1964.

The British Invasion of Rock Music

Rock and roll music began in the United States. Musicians such as Elvis Presley and Chuck Berry pioneered it. In the 1960s, several bands from Britain took the lead. Their songs swept across America and changed rock music forever. Music fans called it the British Invasion.

The Beatles started the British Invasion. They were a group of four young men from Liverpool, England. John Lennon and Paul McCartney wrote most of the band's songs. George Harrison played guitar. Ringo Starr was the group's drummer. The Beatles first became famous in Britain. They played hit tunes like "Love Me Do" and "I Want to Hold Your Hand." In February 1964, they appeared on American television. Over 70 million people saw them perform on *The Ed Sullivan Show*. The Beatles went on to become the most influential rock band ever.

Ed Sullivan (center) stands with the Beatles (from left, Ringo Starr, George Harrison, John Lennon, and Paul McCartney), 1964. The band's appearance on *The Ed Sullivan Show* made them stars in the United States.

The Rolling Stones were also hugely popular. Singer Mick Jagger and guitarist Keith Richards led the band. The early hits of the Rolling Stones included "Time Is on My Side" and "Satisfaction." The Beatles broke up in 1970. However, the Rolling Stones continued making new music for decades.

CIVIL RIGHTS MOVEMENT SUCCEEDS

The civil rights movement was a long struggle for racial equality. Its leaders focused on the American South. Segregation laws there kept blacks separate from the rest of society. Other laws denied African Americans the right to vote.

In the 1960s, black people actively fought to change these laws. They marched through the streets in protest. They also staged "sit-ins," going to whites-only restaurants and sitting at a table or lunch counter until they were

Many whites joined African Americans in the August 1963 March on Washington for Jobs and Freedom.

At the end of the March on Washington, Martin Luther King, Jr., delivered a famous speech. "I have a dream that one day this nation will rise up and live out the true meaning of its creed: 'We hold these truths to be self-evident, that all men are created equal,'" he told a crowd of more than 250,000 people, August 28, 1963.

served or arrested. Sometimes, violence erupted between the protesters and their opponents. The nation saw these shocking scenes on television. It helped build support for the protesters' cause.

Martin Luther King, Jr., was a well-known civil rights leader. He preached peaceful protest. In August 1963, King spoke before a crowd of more than two hundred thousand people in Washington, D.C. He told them, "I have a dream that my four little children will one day live in a nation where they will not be judged by the color of their skin but by the content of their character." King's moving speech was a turning point in the civil rights movement.

The protests began to work. In 1964, President Lyndon Johnson signed into law federal legislation to end segregation. A year later, another federal law helped ensure that blacks would not be denied the right to vote. The civil rights movement was succeeding.

President Lyndon B. Johnson prepares to sign the Civil Rights Act, July 1964. This law made it illegal to prevent African Americans and members of any other racial group from hotels, theaters, restaurants, and all other public places. It also outlawed discrimination against minorities in the workplace.

TRAGEDY IN THE SPACE RACE

America and the Soviet Union both wished to be the first to the moon. Each nation rushed to take the lead in the space race. They soon discovered the perils of space exploration.

Spacecraft are complex machines. They contain many wires and other parts that can spark a fire. In 1961, tragedy struck the Soviet space program. A sudden fire killed a cosmonaut. Six years later, the U.S. space program suffered a similar disaster. Three astronauts died from fire while in training. Their names were Virgil "Gus" Grissom, Edward White, and Roger Chaffee.

The second stage engine of a massive Saturn V rocket is hoisted into place, January 1967. The Apollo 1 astronauts were training to make the first flight into space powered by this complex 364-foot-tall rocket.

Shortly after this photo was taken, astronauts Virgil I. "Gus" Grissom, Edward H. White, and Roger B. Chaffee were killed in the Apollo 1 fire.

The three men were training for the Apollo 1 mission. Their job was to test the spacecraft that would someday go to the moon. On January 27, 1967, they were practicing in their space capsule as it sat on the launch pad. Suddenly, the capsule filled with flames. The astronauts were trapped. They died before help could arrive.

Grissom, White, and Chaffee did not die in vain. NASA, the agency in charge of the U.S. space program, improved the design of the space capsule. It became much safer. No astronauts died in any of the Apollo missions that followed.

This photo shows the charred exterior of the Apollo 1 capsule. The deadly fire set back America's space program for a year, as NASA tried to determine what had gone wrong.

Tragedy in the Space Race

Israeli soldiers stand at the Western Wall, part of the ancient Jewish temple, after capturing Jerusalem from Jordanian forces in June 1967.

Six-Day War Rocks the Middle East

The Middle East has long been a troubled region. One major source of that trouble is the Arab-Israeli conflict. Since the 1940s, the Jewish state of Israel and its Arab neighbors have clashed. In June 1967, the two sides fought a brief but important war. It is remembered today as the Six-Day War.

A column of Israeli tanks on the Sinai Peninsula, June 1967. Israel captured this vast desert territory from Egypt during the Six-Day War.

Israel was created after World War II. During that war, Nazi Germany killed nearly 6 million European Jews. The wide-scale slaughter became known as the Holocaust. Afterward, Jewish people wanted a country of their own. It would be a place of safety for Holocaust survivors and other Jews. Many countries, including the United States, supported the creation of a Jewish state in Palestine. This is a region in the Middle East where a Jewish kingdom had existed thousands of years ago.

But there was a problem. Arab people had been living in Palestine for more than a thousand years. Most of them were Muslims, or people who follow the religion of Islam. They did not want a Jewish state in their midst, and on land they considered theirs.

In May 1948, the Jewish state of Israel was officially established. Almost immediately, the surrounding Arab countries attacked it. They tried to destroy the new Jewish state, but failed. Tension remained high between Israel and the Arab states for decades. Occasionally, fierce fighting broke out.

In 1967, the Arab countries of Egypt, Jordan, and Syria planned to attack Israel. But Israel did not wait. It struck first. On June 5, 1967, Israeli jets bombed Egypt. They wiped out the Egyptian air force. Waves of Israeli soldiers also attacked. They seized land belonging to Egypt. The Israeli troops also pushed back the armies of Jordan and Syria. Startled Arab soldiers retreated in chaos. By June 10, the war was over. Israel had scored a swift and thorough victory.

The Arab nations were stunned by their defeat. Roughly eighteen thousand Arab soldiers died in the fighting. Meanwhile, Israel lost just seven hundred of its troops. It also captured large areas of land. The Arab states vowed to keep fighting Israel. They also pledged to someday regain their lost ground. In just six years, Egypt and Syria would once again go to war with Israel. Both sides would suffer heavy losses but not resolve their differences. To this day, the Arab-Israeli conflict remains a cause of concern for the world.

Israel's flag flies over a captured gun emplacement on the Golan Heights, which Israeli troops seized from Syria.

Boxing Champ Fights Controversy

Many people consider Muhammad Ali the greatest boxer of all time. Ali was born in Kentucky in 1942. His parents named him Cassius Clay. He changed his name to Muhammad Ali in 1964 for religious reasons. By that time, he was already a world-famous boxer. He had won an Olympic gold medal, plus nineteen pro matches.

Ali was proud and confident. He often boasted about his boxing skills. He liked to say that he could float like a butterfly, and sting like a bee. In 1964, Ali took on heavyweight champion Sonny Liston. He soundly beat Liston to become the new champ. Ali defended his title many times.

Muhammad Ali glares at Sonny Liston after knocking him down during a 1965 fight for the heavyweight championship. Ali had won the heavyweight title from Liston the previous year, and held it until 1967.

Ali speaks to reporters on his way into a Houston, Texas, court to face trial because of his refusal to be drafted into the U.S. Army, June 20, 1967. He was found guilty and sentenced to 5 years in prison (a conviction that was eventually overturned in 1971).

In 1967, Muhammad Ali became the center of controversy. He refused to go into the U.S. Army. At the time, young men were being drafted into the military to fight in Vietnam. However, Ali said that he could not fight in the Vietnam War. He felt it was morally wrong. Ali's refusal cost him his boxing title.

In 1970, Ali returned to the ring. He regained the world heavyweight title in 1974 by knocking out George Foreman.

Muhammad Ali punches Jerry Quarry during his first fight after being suspended, October 26, 1970, in Atlanta, Georgia. Ali ended his fighting career in 1981, after winning fifty-six of sixty-one fights. He won the world heavyweight championship three times.

Boxing Champ Fights Controversy

THE TET OFFENSIVE SHOCKS AMERICANS

The United States was drawn into the war in Vietnam gradually. During the 1950s, American leaders feared that if South Vietnam became communist, the rest of Southeast Asia would follow. Americans called this idea the "domino theory" because they believed that, like dominoes standing in a line, the countries of the region would all fall if one of them were knocked over. To prevent South Vietnam from falling to communism, the United States helped put an anticommunist ruler in power there in the 1950s. In the early 1960s, the United States sent military advisers to help the South Vietnamese army fight communist guerrillas. Eventually, some of these advisers were pulled into actual fighting. Then, in August 1964, U.S. warships off the coast of North Vietnam reported being attacked by North Vietnamese vessels. The Tonkin Gulf incident, as it came to be called, angered Americans. President Johnson used the incident to get Congress to approve whatever measures the president thought necessary to prevent further aggression. In early 1965, American warplanes began bombing North Vietnam. Soon, large numbers of American troops were sent to South Vietnam. By the end of

President Lyndon B. Johnson greets American troops in Vietnam, 1966. After Johnson became president in 1963, he greatly increased U.S. involvement in the Vietnam War. By the time Johnson left office in January 1969, more than half a million U.S. soldiers were fighting in Vietnam.

Wounded marines receive emergency care during a 1968 battle. Television news reports showing Americans dying in battle helped to turn many people against the Vietnam War.

1965, more than 180,000 American soldiers were in that country. They fought Vietcong guerrillas and soldiers from the North Vietnamese army.

By late 1967, the American public was evenly divided over the war in Vietnam. Many people believed the United States should never have gotten involved in the war. But many others thought fighting in Vietnam was the right thing to do. They also believed President Lyndon Johnson and his advisers, who insisted that the United States was winning the war. That would change in 1968.

In January 1968, communist forces launched a massive surprise attack. They struck in cities all across South Vietnam. The campaign was dubbed the Tet Offensive because it started during the Vietnamese New Year, or Tet.

U.S. and South Vietnamese forces were caught off guard. Even so, they slowly regained control of the cities. Most of the North Vietnamese and Vietcong attackers were killed.

Still, the Tet Offensive shocked Americans. It suddenly did not seem that the war was going well. Americans saw images of the bloody fighting on television. The brutal scenes horrified them. After Tet, public opinion began turning against the war.

Vietnamese citizens flee from Hue during the Tet Offensive. They crossed the Perfume River on a bridge that was blown up by the Vietcong.

FAMOUS LEADERS ASSASSINATED

In 1968, two famous American leaders were killed. They were both shot by assassins. The murders shocked the nation.

On April 4, 1968, Martin Luther King, Jr., was in Memphis, Tennessee. King was supporting city workers who were on strike. That evening, the civil rights leader was standing outside his motel room. He was shot in the head by a sniper. King died almost instantly. The world mourned his passing. In the following days, black citizens outraged by King's murder rioted in more than a hundred U.S. cities. America seemed to be tearing itself apart. King's killer was caught two months later. He was an escaped white convict named James Earl Ray. He spent the rest of his life in prison.

Robert F. Kennedy was the brother of President John Kennedy. He was a lawyer and politician. When his brother was president, Robert Kennedy served as U.S. attorney general. He then became

Martin Luther King, Jr.'s death enraged many people. In the days after King was assassinated, riots erupted in more than a hundred cities. Most of the riots started in African-American neighborhoods. They caused about $50 million in damage. This photo shows a National Guardsman watching for trouble while firemen attempt to put out a fire set by rioters in Washington, D.C., April 6, 1968.

Robert Kennedy (1925–1968) speaks at a rally, circa 1965. Many African Americans admired Kennedy for his work on civil rights legislation. Young people supported Kennedy's campaign for president because he wanted to end the Vietnam War.

a senator from New York. In 1968, Robert Kennedy decided to run for president. On June 5, he was leaving a campaign event in Los Angeles. An assassin suddenly leapt out and shot him. Kennedy died the following day. He was forty-two years old. Kennedy's killer, Sirhan Sirhan, was sentenced to life imprisonment.

In 1983, U.S. President Ronald Reagan signed a bill making Martin Luther King, Jr.'s birthday a federal holiday. King's wife, Coretta Scott King, stands at the president's side. Martin Luther King Jr. Day was first observed on January 20, 1986. Today, the holiday occurs on the third Monday of each January.

Residents of Prague, carrying a Czechoslovakian flag and throwing burning torches, attempt to stop a Soviet tank, August 21,1968.

SOVIET TANKS CRUSH THE PRAGUE SPRING

After World War II, the Soviet Union took control of many nearby countries. The Soviets forced communism on their smaller neighbors. Czechoslovakia was one of these nations. By the 1960s, the Czech people were tired of Soviet communism. They wanted to try something new. They sought to change the communist system. Their attempt became known as the Prague Spring.

Prague was the capital of Czechoslovakia. Leaders of Czech society met there to talk about making reforms. The leaders included politicians, writers, economists, and artists. They felt that Soviet communism did not work well for Czechoslovakia. Many of the country's citizens were poor and unhappy. They needed better jobs. They also wanted more freedom.

After gaining control of Czechoslovakia's Communist Party in early 1968, Alexander Dubcek (1921–1992) pushed for greater freedom.

The Czech leaders planned sweeping changes. They thought of ways to enhance the nation's economy. They also agreed to limit the power of the government. It would no longer be able to control the newspapers. People would be permitted to speak freely. They could talk about politics. They could even criticize the government if they wished. The reformers did not plan to abandon communism. They simply wanted to improve upon it.

The Prague Spring posed a problem for Leonid Brezhnev. He had replaced Nikita Khrushchev as the leader of the Soviet Union. Brezhnev did not want to lose control of Czechoslovakia. He also feared that other countries the Soviet Union controlled might be inspired by Czechoslovakia. They, too, might try

When the Czech government refused to end its reform program, Soviet leader Leonid I. Brezhnev (1906–1982) sent the Red Army to seize control of the country. The Soviet Union's allies—Bulgaria, East Germany, Hungary, and Poland— also participated in the invasion.

A huge crowd of Czechs protest against the Soviet invasion at Wenceslas Square in Prague, Czechoslovakia, August 1968.

making reforms. Brezhnev saw the Prague Spring as a threat to the entire Soviet Union. He warned the Czechs to stop their reforms. They refused.

In August 1968, Soviet troops and tanks stormed into Czechoslovakia. They took control of the Czech government. They abolished the Prague Spring reforms. The Czech people were angry. They marched in protest. Eventually, though, they came to accept that the Prague Spring was over. Life under Soviet communism returned to normal.

The Prague Spring drew worldwide attention. It showed that the Soviet leaders would use force to keep their empire intact. However, later events proved that the Czechs were right. Gradually, it became clear that Soviet communism would fail everywhere. In the 1980s, the Soviet Union adopted many of the reforms from the Prague Spring.

HERE COME THE HIPPIES

Hippie culture arose in the 1960s. Hippies were young people who rejected the values of society. They strongly opposed the Vietnam War. They preached love and peace as answers to the world's problems. They also believed in protecting nature and the environment. Hippies had a unique style. They wore their hair long and dressed in colorful clothing. Beads and headbands were very popular.

Older Americans found hippie culture alarming. Many hippies chose not to work. They preferred to listen to music and use illegal drugs. Some of them lived on communes with other hippies. Others traveled around the country on foot or by hitchhiking. Hippies did not care about having goods or money. They often relied on the charity of others. Hippie customs defied traditional American values.

San Francisco was the heart of the hippie movement. In the summer of 1967, more

Hippies dance at a "love-in," or public gathering. During the late 1960s, love-ins were held as protests against war or environmental problems. Hippies often dressed in bright clothing and wore flowers in their hair. They used the phrase "flower power" to describe their gentle, peace-seeking philosophy.

than 100,000 hippies and people who were attracted by hippie culture gathered in the city. They dubbed it the "Summer of Love." Two years later, half a million young people gathered in rural New York. They attended the Woodstock Music and Art Fair. It featured many famous singers and music groups, including such hippie favorites as the Grateful Dead, Jefferson Airplane, Janis Joplin, and Jimi Hendrix. Woodstock was considered the ultimate hippie experience, even though many of the people in attendance were not actually hippies.

An enormous crowd enjoys the music during the Woodstock festival in August 1969. About four hundred thousand people came to a small village in rural New York for the show, which was billed as "three days of peace and music."

Astronaut Edwin E. "Buzz" Aldrin stands beside the U.S. flag during the Apollo 11 mission, July 20, 1969. The two American astronauts spent twenty-two hours on the lunar surface.

Humans Set Foot on the Moon

The 1960s had been a turbulent decade. It was marked by tragedy and conflict. Yet the decade ended on an uplifting note. In July 1969, humans first set foot on the moon. The men who walked on the moon were American. However, they took their steps on behalf of all humanity. People around the globe celebrated the amazing feat. For a brief moment, the troubles of the world were forgotten.

America's space program overcame many challenges. For years, it trailed behind the Soviet space program. In 1967, it endured tragedy when three astronauts died on the launch pad. However, the men and women of NASA

Dr. Wernher von Braun (1912–1977) poses in front of the enormous Saturn V rocket that would carry the Apollo 11 astronauts to the moon. Braun directed the American rocket program during the 1950s and 1960s. He has been called the "father of the American space program."

did not waver. They learned from their mistakes. By 1969, they were ready to attempt a mission to land astronauts on the moon. The mission was called Apollo 11. Three astronauts were chosen for the job. Their names were Neil Armstrong, Michael Collins, and Edwin "Buzz" Aldrin.

The Apollo 11 spacecraft blasted off on July 16, 1969. Four days later, it was in orbit around the moon. A landing craft called *Eagle* was attached to the main ship, *Columbia*. Aldrin and Armstrong climbed into *Eagle*. Collins stayed behind to pilot *Columbia*. *Eagle* slowly began its descent toward the moon's surface. Armstrong guided it to a safe landing zone. He had to avoid craters and boulders. *Eagle* touched down on a plain known as the Sea of Tranquility.

The Apollo 11 crew included (from left) mission commander Neil A. Armstrong, Michael Collins, and Buzz Aldrin.

Earth can be seen in the background of this photograph of *Eagle*, the tiny craft that carried Neil Armstrong and Buzz Aldrin to the moon. Michael Collins took this photo from *Columbia* on July 20, 1969.

Neil Armstrong was the first person to set foot on the moon. As he did so, he stated, "That's one small step for [a] man, one giant leap for mankind." Buzz Aldrin came out next. The two astronauts explored the lunar surface. Its gray dust felt like snow under their boots. They collected rocks to take back to Earth. They also set up experiments. After twenty-one hours, *Eagle* lifted off from the moon. Armstrong and Aldrin rejoined Collins in the main ship. They began the long journey home.

The astronauts returned to Earth as heroes. They described their experiences to the public. Scientists analyzed the moon rocks they brought back. Over the next three years, NASA launched five more manned lunar missions. The last person to stand on the moon was Eugene Cernan in 1972.

LOOKING AHEAD

Breaking free from one's parents is a natural part of growing up. But many young people who came of age during the 1960s were especially vocal in rejecting the values of their elders. Rather than accepting the traditional paths of career and family, they said they wanted to "tune in, turn on, and drop out" of society. They used illegal drugs. They supported "free love." They condemned the war in Vietnam and rebelled against authority. Their attitude was summed up by a popular saying: "Never trust anyone over thirty."

This attitude, like the Vietnam War, lingered into the early years of the 1970s. During that time, however, increasing numbers of older Americans also found reason to distrust people in positions of authority. In 1971, top-secret government files that were leaked to the press showed that U.S. leaders had told a series of lies about the Vietnam War. Three years later, after a long political scandal, an American president would be forced to resign.

As the 1970s progressed, the country would suffer more blows to its prestige. Some Americans began to wonder whether the nation was in decline. If the 1960s had been a youth-driven period of social and cultural upheaval, the 1970s would be a more sober time of self-doubt.

During the 1970s, women fought for greater acceptance and equality in the workplace. Supporters of the Women's Liberation movement believed that women and men should be paid the same salaries if they performed the same work.

CHRONOLOGY

1960—The Soviet Union shoots down an American U-2 spy plane. In November, John F. Kennedy becomes the youngest person ever elected U.S. president.

1961—Cosmonaut Yuri Gagarin becomes the first person in space, on April 12. Five days later, the Bay of Pigs invasion fails in Cuba.

1962—In Britain, the Beatles sign their first record contract. Astronaut John Glenn becomes the first American to orbit Earth. In October, the Cuban Missile Crisis pushes the world to the brink of nuclear war.

1963—Martin Luther King, Jr., delivers his "I Have a Dream" speech in August. President Kennedy is assassinated on November 22. Accused assassin Lee Harvey Oswald is shot and killed two days later.

1964—King receives the Nobel Peace Prize. The Beatles make their first appearance on American television in February. Boxer Muhammad Ali defeats Sonny Liston to become the world heavyweight champion.

1965—U.S. forces begin to take a leading role in the Vietnam War. Congress passes the Voting Rights Act, which bans southern laws designed to keep black people from voting.

1966—Large-scale protests of the Vietnam War begin. Hippie culture grows and spreads across the nation.

1967—In January, three U.S. astronauts die in a training accident. In June, the Six-Day War breaks out in the Middle East. Muhammad Ali is stripped of his boxing title for refusing to enter the U.S. Army.

1968—Martin Luther King, Jr., is assassinated on April 4. Presidential candidate Robert F. Kennedy is assassinated two months later. Soviet forces crush the Prague Spring in August.

1969—On July 20, astronauts Neil Armstrong and Buzz Aldrin become the first humans to walk on the moon. In August, half a million people attend the Woodstock rock festival in rural New York.

GLOSSARY

assassination—The murder of a well-known person for political or other reasons.

Cold War—A long struggle between the United States and the Soviet Union that stopped short of full-scale war.

communism—A type of political and economic system in which all citizens are supposed to share work and property equally.

cosmonaut—A Russian or Soviet astronaut.

economist—A person who studies the flow of goods and money in society.

guerrilla—Warfare involving small groups of soldiers who stage surprise raids.

lunar—Relating to the moon.

Muslim—A believer in the religion of Islam.

NASA—Short for the National Aeronautics and Space Administration, it is America's space agency.

nuclear weapon—An incredibly powerful bomb that releases atomic energy.

protest—An act or statement that expresses strong disagreement.

satellite—An orbiting object in space.

sniper—Someone who shoots a rifle from a concealed position.

spy plane—A high-flying aircraft used to study enemy activity.

superpower—A powerful nation that leads other nations.

FURTHER READING

Aronson, Marc. *Up Close: Robert F. Kennedy*. New York: Viking Juvenile, 2007.

Byrne, Paul. J. *The Cuban Missile Crisis: To the Brink of War*. Mankato, Minn.: Compass Point Books, 2006.

Cullen, David. *The First Man in Space*. Milwaukee, Wis.: World Almanac Library, 2004.

Golus, Carrie. *Muhammad Ali*. Minneapolis, Minn.: Twenty-First Century Books, 2006.

Kaplan, Howard S. *John F. Kennedy*. New York: DK Publishing, 2004.

Levy, Debbie. *The Vietnam War*. Minneapolis, Minn.: Lerner Publications, 2004.

Pastan, Amy. *Martin Luther King, Jr*. New York: DK Publishing, 2004.

Spitz, Bob. *Yeah! Yeah! Yeah!: The Beatles, Beatlemania, and the Music That Changed the World*. New York: Little, Brown Books for Young Readers, 2007.

Thimmesh, Catherine. *Team Moon: How 400,000 People Landed Apollo 11 on the Moon*. New York: Houghton Mifflin, 2006.

INTERNET RESOURCES

<http://www.gwu.edu/~nsarchiv/nsa/cuba_mis_cri/>
George Washington University offers this study of the Cuban Missile Crisis. See documents that were once top secret. Hear President Kennedy discuss the crisis with his advisers.

<http://www.nps.gov/history/nr/travel/civilrights/>
This site is from the National Park Service. It highlights important places during the civil rights movement. Find out if a civil rights landmark is near you.

<http://www.thebeatles.com/core/home/>
Visit the official Web site of the Beatles. Learn the fascinating story of the world's most famous rock and roll band.

Index

PICTURE CREDITS